White Feathers

Stephanie Baudet

Published by the Press Syndicate of the University of Cambridge,
The Pitt Building, Trumpington Street, Cambridge CB2 1RP
40 West 20th Street, New York, NY 10011-4211, USA
10 Stamford Road, Oakleigh, Melbourne 3166, Australia

First published 1993
Printed in Great Britain at the University Press, Cambridge
A catalogue record for this book is available from the British Library

ISBN 0 521 45636 3
Illustrated by Liz Roberts
Prepared by *specialist publishing services* 090 857 307

Other titles in the *Moonstones* series include:

The author

Stephanie Baudet was born in Cheshire in 1945 but spent most of her childhood in Australia and New Zealand where she trained as a nurse before returning to England in 1967. She now lives in Buckinghamshire with her husband and two cats and has a grown-up daughter who lives in Switzerland. Stephanie has written a number of books for children.

Chapter 1

The back door creaked and Chris smiled to herself. It was just like something out of a horror film. Old house, creaking door – next there'd be the cobwebs and then the thunderstorm.

She'd been surprised to find the door unlocked and, looking round, could see that she wasn't the first to enter uninvited. Others had left the inevitable trail of litter behind them. Well, it wasn't really trespassing, was it? The old place was going to be demolished she'd heard.

She went through into the hall and looked up the stairs. It had been right up at the top, that window, looked like an attic. She began to climb, carefully, but the stairs creaked. On the first landing there was a smaller staircase which must surely lead to the attic room. Chris tiptoed up and very gently opened the door, relieved that this one was silent.

It was a dimly lit room with only the one small window and it took a few seconds for her eyes to grow accustomed to the gloom. Then she saw them. Two white ghostly shapes, staring at her with large unblinking eyes from a shelf in the corner.

Chris slowly entered the room. "You lovely creatures," she breathed. The owls watched her every move, just turning their heads slightly.

"Don't worry, I won't come too close," she said, softly. "I just came to see if you had any babies."

She could see now that there were two fluffy white young in the nest. Two baby barn owls.

3

While Chris was still savouring her discovery she heard a creaking noise below. She froze, staring at the open door. Her heart thudded and she felt a cold sweat break out on her face as the creaking was accompanied by footsteps. Someone was coming up the stairs!

She looked round. There was nowhere to hide, the room was bare and, besides, any quick movement would frighten the owls. Even now, the owls came foremost in her mind.

The footsteps had reached the landing and stopped briefly. Now they started again and began to climb the stairs towards the attic. Chris couldn't move. She felt sick and dizzy, and her mouth went dry as she stared into the dimness beyond the door. She was trapped here, completely trapped. No one would hear her if she screamed…

A boy's head appeared – and then the rest of him. She vaguely recognised him from school. He was in a class below her. Relief flooded over her but she tried to look nonchalant.

"Who are you?" she demanded, trying to sound authoritative but still keeping her voice quiet.

"Steve," answered the boy in a loud voice. "You're the new girl in Mr Lewis' class, aren't you?" He stopped in surprise as she made frantic gestures for him to be quiet.

"Why should I keep quiet?" he said. "This isn't your house. What are you doing here, anyway?"

"What are *you* doing here?"

"I saw you come in and I followed. They're going to demolish this house pretty soon."

Chris turned round to look at the owls again and Steve followed her gaze. He gasped. "What are they?"

"They're barn owls, and they have two babies. That's why I came in. I've seen them flying in and out of the window and I thought they must have a nest here."

Steve didn't look very interested. "Not much of a nest," he said. "What'll happen when they knock the house down?"

"I hope they'll be able to fly by then and will have left the nest."

Steve strode forward. "Let's have a look."

"No!" Chris took a step sideways, tripped over something and fell heavily against the wall which made a dull cracking noise. She struggled to her feet and faced him angrily.

"You'll frighten them!" she hissed. She looked at the owls. They were clacking their beaks and obviously agitated but weren't going to leave their young.

Steve just grinned, looking past her at the wall. "You've smashed the wall in," he said. "It's all caved in behind the wallpaper."

She looked at it, briefly, more concerned about the birds.

"Let's go," she said.

Steve shrugged and turned to the door and she followed him though it and down the stairs.

"Horrible old place," he said as they reached the landing. "I was always too scared to come here before."

"Why?"

"The old man who lived here, Mr Bingley, he was weird."

"What happened to him?"

"He's gone to live at Green Park – you know – the old people's home."

"Oh." Chris closed the back door behind her.

"See yer," said Steve, sauntering off with his hands in his jeans pockets.

"Wait!" called Chris and ran to catch him up. "Don't tell anyone about the owls, will you?"

"Why not?"

"Because everyone would be going up to see them and I don't know what would happen."

"Who cares?" said Steve, and turned out of the gate and along the path leaving her standing staring after him.

Who cares? She did. And she hoped fervently that the demolition wasn't too soon. She had no idea how long it was before baby owls could fly but she was going to find out.

She went to see them again the next day, taking care that no one saw her enter the house. The owls seemed quite calm but watchful; it was the babies who were restless and making their hissing snoring noise. Chris smiled, still keeping her distance. She was about to turn and leave when she noticed the wall where she'd fallen against it. How odd that it had caved in like that!

She poked at the wallpaper and her finger went right through it, so she carefully tore it away. Concealed behind was the remains of a wooden cupboard, the door of which was now broken.

Intrigued, Chris pulled out the broken pieces of rotten wood until the whole of the inside was exposed. There was something inside. Two things in fact. She reached in and lifted out a large bundle of papers. They were letters. Letters written in faded ink and tied together with string. Why had they been hidden in a cupboard and then papered over?

Chris looked more closely at the letters. The name and address on the envelopes was so faded she couldn't read it. They were certainly very old. Placing them back into the cupboard she looked again at the other thing. It was a huge metal object, sort of pear-shaped with some metal framework on top. She grasped it but it wouldn't move. Whatever it was, it was very heavy. Chris replaced the broken pieces of cupboard door as best she could and left. She'd have a look at those letters another time, but in the meantime she didn't want anyone else snooping around.

As she left, she noticed that there was a key in the attic door. She locked it and hid the key in a dark corner behind the bannister post. That would keep them out. She didn't trust that Steve at all.

He sidled over to her during the lunch break at school the next day.

"Going to visit the owls today?" he grinned. Chris looked at him. His lively brown eyes seemed to show genuine interest without a hint of mockery.

"Might," she said.

"Doesn't it worry you being alone in that house?"

"No, 'course not. Why should it?"

"That funny old man lived there all those years."

"So? Why was he funny, anyhow?"

"He talks to himself," said Steve, "and acts funny. My mum says she was always told to keep away when she was a little girl. You never know what he might do."

"He must be very old," said Chris.

"He's more than ninety."

"Who's more than ninety?"

They turned to see Sarah Gordon from Chris's class standing behind them. She flicked her head causing her pale, corn-coloured hair to shimmer, and grinned at them both.

"Old Mr Bingley," said Steve.

"Weird," said Sarah. "Why are you talking about him, for goodness sake?"

"Chris wondered who the old house belonged to," said Steve with a mischievous glint in his eyes.

"I heard that it was going to be demolished, that's all," said Chris, quickly.

"And a good job too," said Sarah. "What a dump! He never did anything to it all his life, my dad says. Never went anywhere, just stayed at home. No wonder he went mad."

"Just because you talk to yourself doesn't mean you're mad," said Chris.

"Why, do you talk to *your*self?" laughed Sarah, flicking her head again. "I bet you do but won't admit it!"

"I don't!"

"It's all nonsense though," put in Steve. "He goes on about Zeppelins and bombs and things."

"What are Zeppelins?" asked Chris.

"Great big airships that the Germans used in the war to fly over and drop bombs."

"Oh, listen to him!" mocked Sarah. "Know-all Steven. What a boring pair you are!" She spun round and strode off to join another group.

"Cow!" said Steve, and he strolled away too leaving Chris on her own.

Nothing's changed, she thought. Life at her old school had been misery. Here, her problems hadn't even started yet but it wasn't looking very promising. So what! She'd survive as she always had. For a moment she felt a flash of sympathy for old Mr Bingley. Poor, lonely Mr Bingley. No wonder he talked to himself.

It looked thundery as she walked home that afternoon. It had become very dark and gloomy and she felt a few spots of rain on her face as she turned into her road.

"You're not going out again, are you Chris?" said her mum, seeing her in the hall with a jacket on over her jeans.

"It looks as though we're in for a storm."

"I'm not afraid of storms," said Chris.

Her mother didn't look convinced. She peered closely at her. "Are you all right? Where are you going?"

"Not far," said Chris, evasively. "I'll be indoors." And went before her mother could raise any objections. She grinned to herself, wondering what her mother would have said if she'd replied: "I'm going to that house where a mad old man lived, to see some owls."

The key was where she'd left it, of course, and she let herself in quietly. Both parent owls were there with their babies as usual, as if they never left their sides, but Chris knew that at night one or other of them went off foraging for food to bring back.

The rain was becoming heavier now and beat loudly on the roof above her head. Chris pulled away the broken cupboard door, took out the bundle of letters and went over to perch on the window sill. She took the first letter out of its envelope, unfolded the dry sheets of paper carefully and began to read:

26 Brownlow Street,
London, SE4

26th April 1914

Dear Ron,
I can't wait to tell you! I got a ticket for the Cup Final last night at Crystal Palace! You'll know the result now, of course, Burnley beat Liverpool one nil. You should have been here! What a match!

How's life there? Quiet by comparison, I imagine. Mother's deeply involved in this suffragette movement and good luck to them, I say, although I don't hold with this smashing up cabinets in the British Museum and slashing priceless paintings. Mother nearly got arrested herself last week!

9

*Do write and let me know your news. Why don't you come
and stay for a while, or can't your mother be left? Sorry to hear
she's ill.*

*Do you think there's going to be a war in Europe? If we're
involved I shall be the first to sign up! If your mother's well we
can sign up together! Nancy says 'hello'. Weren't you sweet on
her? Come and stay as soon as you can and we'll all three have a
jolly good time!*

Regards from your old friend,
Stanley

Chris carefully put the letter back into its envelope. It
sounded very old fashioned. She wondered who Ron and
Stanley were, and what they were like. They'd be very old
now if they were still alive. Did Ron ever go and stay with
Stanley in London, and who was Nancy? Perhaps they got
married in the end. Maybe the other letters would tell her.

She couldn't read any more now, the light was too bad
and the writing faint and spidery. She must remember to
bring a torch or something tomorrow.

It was really pouring as she let herself out of the door of
the house and ran home.

"I knew you'd get soaked," said her mum as she burst
through the back door and dripped all over the floor. "Leave
your shoes there and then get the rest of your wet things off."

"What's a suffragette?" asked Chris as she changed into
dry clothes.

"A sort of women's libber," said her mum, "campaigning
for women to have the right to vote. That was a long time
ago. Where did you hear about it?"

"Oh, I read it somewhere," said Chris. "Did they really
smash things up and get arrested?"

Her mum nodded. "They used to chain themselves to
railings and hold demonstrations and were often put in

11

prison. Then they'd go on hunger strikes and refuse to eat."

"How awful." She wondered whether it had ever happened to Stanley's mother.

"Cauliflower cheese all right for your dinner?"

"Yes, please."

Her mum glanced out of the window.

"Then you'll have to pop up to the shop for a cauliflower. The rain seems to have stopped for the moment. Take my umbrella."

She saw the look on Chris's face.

"You're the one who's difficult with meals."

Chris took the pound coin her mum held out to her and went out. It wasn't being difficult, being vegetarian, she just felt strongly about not eating dead animals. Like the suffragettes felt strongly about not being able to vote. She would never smash things up, but chaining herself to railings – that was worth thinking about.

The little supermarket wasn't far and she was soon on the return journey with a splendid white cauliflower in a carrier bag. Just ahead of her a little dog poked its head out of the open gate of the house next to the butcher's and looked at her mischievously.

Chris smiled. "Hello," she said.

The dog wagged its tail and then trotted off along the pavement. At a side road it began to cross without hesitation. Before Chris realised what was happening there was a horrible thud and a car raced out into the main road, its tyres squealing. For a moment she caught the eyes of the young driver as it raced past and then she ran forward to the little furry form which lay motionless in the middle of the road.

Chapter 2

The dog was still alive. Its brown eyes looked up at her as she bent over it, wondering what to do. There was no blood. As she watched and gently stroked its head it began to move and try to get to its feet.

"Let's get you home," said Chris. She carefully inserted both hands underneath to support its body and lifted it slowly from the road. Fortunately it was a small dog and easy to carry, though when she reached the front door of the house she had no hands free to ring the bell so she had to kick the door lightly. A man answered.

"Your dog was run over," said Chris, "but the car just drove off."

The man looked angry as he gently took the dog from Chris's arms.

"Where did it happen? What sort of car was it?" he asked.

How should she know? "From the side road," she said, "it was a red car and the driver looked young."

"I bet!" He stroked the dog soothingly. "Thank you for rescuing him. Someone must have left the gate open. How did you know he lived here?"

"The gate was open – I saw him run out."

Just then there was a squeal behind the man and someone rushed forward. It was Sarah Gordon. She glared at Chris and then wailed when she saw the dog.

"Bobby! What's happened? Is he all right?"

"We'll get the vet to have a look at him," said the man. "Thanks again." He smiled at Chris and shut the door.

"You were a long time," said her mum when she got home. Chris related the story of the dog.

Her mother tutted. "How can anyone just drive on and not stop?" she said. "He could at least have moved it to the side of the road or tried to find the owner. You say it belongs to Mr Gordon, the butcher?"

Chris nodded.

"The driver is supposed to report it to the police, too," continued her mum. "Still, let's hope the dog's all right."

"Sarah Gordon's in my class," said Chris, "so I can ask her, but I don't like her very much."

"Why not?"

Chris shrugged. "She's just not very friendly."

But she made a point of asking Sarah at school next day.

"He's all right. Just bruised and shocked, the vet said." She glared at Chris. "But couldn't you have stopped it? Dad said you saw him running out of our gate."

"None of my business," retorted Chris. "I didn't leave your gate open, did I?"

Sarah said nothing but flounced off.

That's all the thanks I get, thought Chris.

Steve walked home with her that afternoon and she told him about it.

"It was probably her that left the gate open in the first place and she's trying to blame someone else," he said.

"Yeah," said Chris, "I thought that too."

"The driver should have stopped, though."

"Would you have?"

"Of course!" he exclaimed. "I'm not cruel!"

Chris was changing her mind about Steve. He obviously hadn't told anyone about the owls.

"Look, I'm not crazy about animals but I wouldn't hurt them."

Chris made a sudden decision. She'd tell Steve about the letters. She might as well have a friend while she could – it probably wouldn't last long.

"Can you keep a secret?"

He looked at her, his eyes lighting up. "Yeah, what?"

"You remember in the old house when I fell against the wall and it caved in?"

He grinned and nodded.

"Well, behind the wallpaper there was a cupboard with a bundle of old letters inside. I read one last night. It was from someone called Stanley to his friend Ron, written in 1914."

Steve whistled. "Ron Bingley," he said.

"You know him?"

"Yeah, the old man. The daft old man that lived there."

"Oh."

It came as a shock to Chris to realise that the letters belonged to old Mr Bingley. She hadn't thought of that. Now it seemed wrong to be reading something so personal.

"Let's go there now," said Steve, looking enthusiastic.

Chris frowned. "Do you think it's all right, reading his letters? Perhaps we should take them to him?"

"No! He's probably forgotten they're there. It's a long time ago. He must have only been a bit older than us."

Chris still felt a bit guilty as they entered the house and climbed the stairs towards the attic, but her curiosity was

16

very quickly getting the better of her.

The owls seemed to be getting used to their visits now and hardly opened their eyes as they entered. The chicks were quiet too. Chris went to have a close look at them. She wondered whether they were nearly ready to fly.

Steve watched her retrieve the letters from the cupboard. She handed him the first one and let him read it to himself.

"What are suffragettes?" he asked when he'd finished.

Chris smiled and told him what her mother had said.

Steve snorted. "They went to prison and went on hunger strike just to be able to vote? Mad!"

Chris felt slightly annoyed but kept silent. She didn't want to have an argument just now. She opened the second letter and began to read out loud.

September 20th 1914

Dear Ron,
I've done it! I've joined up! My group are training in a building nearby so I can live at home for the moment and we get two shillings a day for board and lodging and a shilling a day pay. We haven't got a full uniform yet but it'll come soon. With all the thousands that have joined up since all this started last month, it's no wonder they haven't got properly organised yet, is it?

All my chums have joined too so I know a lot of them in my group. I know I'm not eighteen yet, but I lied. What does a few months matter?

Didn't we have a smashing time when you came? Nancy still talks about it. Pity it was only for a week. You two seemed to get on so well! Do I hear wedding bells in the distance? Ha Ha!

Anyway, Ron, why haven't you joined up yet? Surely someone can look after your mother? I can't wait to get over there and start hammering the hun. As Lord Kitchener says 'Your country needs you!' Write and let me know when you're

coming and we can go to the recruiting office together. You
might get into our unit then. I look forward to hearing from you,
    Your friend,
    Stanley

"So he did go and stay with Stanley then," said Steve. "I wonder if he joined the army."

"Well, if he did, he survived the war."

"Obviously," said Steve.

"I want to see whether he marries Nancy."

"You would," said Steve, "I'll ask Mum if she remembers a Mrs Bingley."

Chris took a last look at the owls. "I must find out how long it is before they fly the nest," she said. They turned to leave.

"Oh!" she exclaimed, suddenly.

"What?"

"I forgot to show you. There's something else in the cupboard with the letters. Look." Chris opened the cupboard again and stood back to let Steve look inside. "Do you know what it is?"

Steve peered in. "Haven't a clue," he said, trying to move it as she had done. "It's heavy."

They both stared at the object silently for a few moments and then Chris put back the bits of cupboard door. They left the attic and she locked the door again and hid the key.

"You trust me now, then?" said Steve.

Chris just grinned at him. Not only did she have a friend but they had an exciting secret. Things were certainly looking up. If only they could stay this way.

"No school tomorrow. We can come and read more letters," said Steve. "It's like a serial isn't it?"

18

Chris nodded. "We're going to visit my grandparents for the weekend but I don't think we're leaving until tomorrow afternoon."

"Why don't we go skating in the morning, have a burger at the rink and then come here and read a letter?" Steve's brown eyes lit up at the prospect of his idea.

"Skating?"

"Ice skating. Haven't you ever done it?"

"No."

"It's easy, I'll teach you."

Chris frowned. "I'd like to but..."

"What?"

How could she say her mother might not let her? He'd laugh at her and it would all start.

"I'd love to," she laughed suddenly. "But no burger, I'm vegetarian."

"I might have guessed," said Steve, but he didn't laugh. "You can just have chips then."

"Ice skating?" said her mother. "Well, I don't know..."

"I'll be all right," insisted Chris.

"Perhaps I'd better find out..."

"Oh, Mum! I'm twelve! I have to do these things like everyone else! I'm no different! I don't want to be different!"

"Of course you're not! And stop shouting, Christine!"

Hot tears ran down Chris's cheeks and she angrily brushed them away. "You don't know what it's like, being laughed at and called names!" And she ran upstairs to her room and banged the door.

19

Her mum did let her go, though. Thanks to her dad really. He was easier. He didn't fuss over her. So when Steve called for her at ten o'clock she was ready in jeans and a jersey.

It was only a short bus ride to the rink. They paid their entrance and went to hire their skates. Steve helped her put them on and lace them firmly.

"Your ankles will get tired and feel all wobbly," he said, "but after a few times they'll strengthen up."

At first Chris didn't think she'd ever be able to let go of the barrier. She had absolutely no control over her feet and they slid everywhere. The rink was packed. One huge mass of people swirling round in an anticlockwise circle.

Steve went off on his own for a bit and after two very slow circuits of the rink, holding tightly to the barrier, Chris got off and sat down for a rest. Steve was right. Her ankles wouldn't seem to support her any more.

She watched everyone else while the music blared out of the loudspeakers, echoing up into the ceiling high above. She could feel the chill off the ice and huddled up to keep warm.

Steve skidded to a stop in front of her. "Come on, Chris, grab my arm and let's go round a couple of times. Then we'll go and eat."

Chris hesitated for a moment, then she determinedly stood up, stepped gingerly on to the ice and linked arms with Steve.

"Leave go of the edge!"

She let go. It suddenly felt very strange and insecure and she longed to grab for the barrier again but didn't, sliding forwards slowly, first with one foot and then the other. After a little while she seemed to get into a sort of rhythm.

"Yeah!" said Steve, which she took as a word of encouragement.

They were on their second circuit when Chris felt a brisk push from behind and before she realised what was happening both she and Steve were sprawling on the ice. They struggled to their feet, unhurt but embarrassed.

"Someone bumped into me," said Chris, breathlessly. "I'm sorry, Steve." She smoothed her hair and pushed it behind her ears.

"Someone pushed you!"

"What do you mean? On purpose?"

"Yes. I saw it happen but couldn't do anything. It was Tony Benson. What has he got against you?"

Chris shrugged. "I don't even know him."

They got off the ice, took off their skates and went up to the cafeteria. Chris sank down on to a chair.

"Just chips?" asked Steve. "Do you want a drink?" She shook her head and he went to the counter.

Chris felt someone approach from behind and she looked up. It was a boy of about fifteen with a shock of straight black hair hanging over his eyes.

"You oughta look where you're going. That could have been a bad fall." He grinned nastily and then leaned forward a little. "Mind you don't poke your nose into other people's business or it might be worse next time."

He sauntered off, leaving Chris staring after him.

"Now what did he want?" asked Steve.

"Who was it?"

"That's Tony Benson, the one who knocked you over."

"He told me not to poke my nose into other people's business. Do you think he knows about the letters?"

"Why should he care about them?"

21

Chris couldn't imagine but it had made her uneasy just the same. She certainly wouldn't go into the old house alone in future – only when Steve was with her.

Perhaps they should take the letters away. But she still wanted to see the owls, and somehow the letters seemed more exciting, read in that house where they'd been hidden for so many years.

"I found out how long it is before baby owls can fly," said Chris as they unlocked the attic door. "Nine to twelve weeks. I phoned the RSPB."

"But how old are they now?" asked Steve.

"That's the trouble, I don't know."

"It hasn't helped much, then. That seems a long time."

"Yes." They went in and looked at the owls.

"What are you going to do if they start knocking the place down?"

Chris shrugged. "We could phone the RSPB. Do you think the builders would delay the demolition until the owls left the nest?"

"It depends, I suppose."

"On what?"

"On how much they care about birds," said Steve.

They opened the cupboard and took out the letters again. Chris walked over to the window and looked out, half expecting to see Tony Benson, but there was no one. Why should it concern him, anyway? Perhaps he'd got her mixed up with someone else.

"They're still at the rink," said Steve, reading her mind. "Hurry up and start reading. Didn't you say you were going to your grandparents' today?"

Chris looked at her watch. "Yes, I haven't got long."

She opened the third letter.

23rd November 1914

Dear Ron,

I say, we were really sorry to hear that your mother had passed away. Our very sincere condolences, old chap. Mother says she hopes you received the wreath she sent.

I've got my posting! We leave for France on 15th December. You're going to miss out on this war if you don't hurry and join up. They say it could be over by Christmas. What a let down if we get there to find it's all over!

What's keeping you, Ron? I thought you were a patriotic sort of chap, King and Country and all that. You always struck me as such. You don't have your poor mother to care for now.

Mother and Nancy are busy knitting socks for the troops. Makes a change from taking part in suffragette rallies! They've also joined a sewing guild at Claridges Hotel to make clothes for servicemen and poor people.

Come on, Ron, do your bit for the country. Nancy says she'll never speak to you again if you don't. She'd be ashamed to call you her friend. There! That should spur you into action if nothing else does!

Wish me luck.
Your friend,
Stanley

Chris folded the letter up. "I must go," she said.

"I wonder why he didn't go to war?" mused Steve.

"Go and ask him," said Chris.

"I might."

"Perhaps he goes later. He was probably upset because his mother had just died. We'll have to wait and see."

"How long did the war last, anyway?"

Chris shrugged. "Long after Christmas, that's for sure. I'll ask Mum."

"What's all this interest in the First World War?" asked her mum.

"Something I'm reading," said Chris.

"History at school, is it?"

"Mmmmm." She mumbled. The war had lasted four years! Certainly long after Christmas.

On Monday she told Chris.

"I know," he said. "But you didn't have to go at the beginning, it was voluntary. In 1916 there was conscription and all men had to go."

"Ron must have gone then?"

He nodded. "Unless he was ill or something."

Chris grinned. "You've been swotting all this up."

"Not on purpose. Once my dad gets started there's no stopping him."

They drifted off to their separate classes. Chris's was biology, usually a subject she enjoyed. Today, however, was different.

"We're going to do some dissecting," anounced Mr Cook. "Sarah's father has kindly let us have a cow's eye."

Sarah Gordon smiled and flicked her hair back.

Everyone gathered round the table except Chris. She watched in horror as Mr Cook opened out the piece of newspaper containing that horrible object. Then she could stand no more and fled from the room.

Chapter 3

Chris ran a little way down the corridor and then stopped. She didn't know where to go or quite what to do next. She looked back towards the classroom door. No one had been sent after her. She had over-reacted a bit, hadn't she? Drawn attention to herself when it would have been better just to quietly refuse to take part and and stay at the back.

She stood, undecided what to do, until boys' voices and loud laughter from the end of the corridor made her hasten towards the classroom door. She didn't want to be caught standing here like an idiot. Then she felt that familiar strange sensation, that warning. Oh no! Not now! The next thing she realised was that the group of older boys were passing her, staring at her, and Tony Benson was among them. He said something and they all laughed.

Chris blinked, shook her head to clear it and then went back into the classroom. Just as well it hadn't been worse.

The whole class looked up as she entered and someone sniggered. Mr Cook peered over the top of his glasses.

"There's no need to run away, Christine. I shan't force you to watch if it upsets you. You can read about the functions of the eye in your textbook."

Chris sat down with relief and opened her book. The diagram didn't look half so bad as she imagined the real thing would.

On the whole, nobody said much about the episode but Steve got to hear of it so it must have been talked about. Mr Cook had been understanding, too, so she probably wasn't the first to be squeamish about dissecting.

Steve teased her a little about it, but not unkindly. "Promise you won't go and read any more letters this afternoon," he said as they walked home. "I've got to go to the dentist."

"OK."

"We'll go tomorrow. Oh, I forgot – do you like swimming?"

"Yes," said Chris, "is there a pool near here?"

"I don't mean the public pool. Paul Jones has got a pool of his own and he's invited a whole lot of us to go on Saturday for a swim. He said you could come too."

"Oh," said Chris.

"What do you mean, Oh," said Steve. "You don't sound very enthusiastic. Can't you swim or something?"

"Yes, of course."

"I mean, do you want to make friends here or not? Everyone says you're a bit stand-offish."

"I'm not!" she retorted, indignantly.

"Well are you coming or not or do you have to ask your mum first?"

There was a slight sneer in his voice and Chris could see that she would lose his friendship if she wasn't careful, and with it the possibility of others.

"Of course not!" she lied. "Will it be warm enough?"

"It's heated," was all he said, and veered off towards his house without another word.

Chris told her mum where she was going on Saturday.

Her mother looked anxious. "Will this boy's parents be there?"

"Of course," said Chris.

"Perhaps I ought to phone them…"

"Oh no! Please, Mum, I'll be all right. I can look after myself. I've been OK for ages." She didn't tell her mum about the time in the school corridor when she'd felt funny.

There was a small parcel for her in the post next day. It was in one of those little padded envelopes with the plastic bubbles which were fun to pop.

Chris sat on the bottom stair in the hall and pulled off the tape at one end, wondering what it could be. It wasn't her birthday.

Inside was an light round object wrapped in a piece of newspaper. How odd! She unwrapped it carefully until it lay exposed in her hand. A large brown cow's eye stared up at her.

Chris screamed, threw the horrid thing away from her and ran into the kitchen.

"Chris! What is it? Whatever is the matter?"

Chris clung to her mother, crying and shaking uncontrollably. "In… the… hall," she said.

"What's in the hall? Is someone there?" She sat Chris on a chair and went to look. Chris heard her picking up the paper and then an exclamation as she found the eye.

"Who's done this?" she demanded, coming back into the kitchen. "Who has sent you this? I shall come and speak to the Head this morning!"

"No, Mum, it'll only make it worse." Chris was recovering a little by now. She told her mother about refusing to dissect an eye in class. "I bet Sarah Gordon did that. She brought the other one to school and this is the sort of thing she would do. She doesn't like me for some reason."

"Never mind, love. You don't need friends like that. You go on this swimming party on Saturday and you'll soon meet some nicer people. Will Steve be there?"

Chris nodded absent-mindedly. She wasn't going to let this thing upset her, in fact, she would just act at school as though nothing had happened. That would disappoint Sarah.

Strangely, Sarah neither spoke to her nor took undue notice of her that day. No hints of any kind were made about the eye and if she'd expected some whispering and giggling as word got around, there was none.

She did tell Steve about it though, and made him promise not to tell anyone. It was good to have someone she could trust and confide in.

He stared at her in horror. "Ugh, how horrible. I don't think even Sarah would do that."

"Who then?"

He shrugged. "Haven't a clue. Who else knew about it?"

"Everyone, probably. You heard about it and you're not in my class."

"True," said Steve. "Anyway, let's go and read some more about Stanley and Ronald. It's strange, isn't it, to think that they're really old men now?"

Chris nodded as they turned into the gate of the old house. It still didn't seem right reading those letters. One day she'd take them back to Ron – Mr Bingley, rather.

The owls allowed them to come closer to their babies now and even Steve smiled as he looked at them.

"They are cute with those big white faces and staring eyes," he said.

"They can't swivel their eyes," said Chris, "that's why they have to turn their heads round."

"I wish my head would turn right round to the back," laughed Steve. "Could be useful."

The fourth letter looked different from the rest and they soon saw why. It was from Nancy. It was written on a fine sort of paper with decorated edges and there was a hint of lavender as Chris opened the sheets. A white feather fell out on to the floor and Steve bent and picked it up.

"What's this?"

"A feather."

"I know that, but what's it doing in the letter?"

Chris shrugged and began to read.

20th December 1914

Dear Ron,

You've really gone down in my estimation. Here you are languishing at home while all those boys – my brother, your friend, included – are fighting for their King and Country in France. I am very disappointed in you. More, I am ashamed to have called you a friend.

The white feather says it all really. You are a coward. You're not alone. My friends and I have given out ten since yesterday morning. Consciencious objectors – is that what you call yourself? It's just an excuse for cowardice.

Ron, I'm sorry it came to this. I had great hopes that our friendship would develop into something more, and so did Stanley, not to mention Mother and Father, but this is the end.

Please do not write to try to explain, I don't want to hear your excuses.

Nancy

"Well!" exclaimed Chris, "what a rotten letter!"

"He deserved it."

"That's not fair! She didn't even give him a chance to explain. He may have had a proper reason for not going to war. Anyway, we know what the white feather was for now. It was given to men who were thought to be cowards." She took the feather from Steve and looked at it, twisting it round in her fingers. "And he kept it all these years."

"So now you know that he never married Nancy," said Steve.

"Yeah, and just as well. I don't like her."

"He did, though, otherwise he wouldn't have kept it. He must have felt ashamed."

They were silent for a moment. What a terrible blow it must have been to get a letter like that, thought Chris, feeling more and more sorry for Ron – Mr Bingley.

She smoothed out the fronds of the feather and carefully put it back into the letter, feeling even more of an intruder into someone else's private affairs. She said so to Steve.

Surprisingly, he nodded. "We'll take them to him later."

"You're not afraid of him any more, then?"

"Not afraid exactly. I feel I know him a bit, but it might still be true that he's a mad. Maybe the shame and disgrace touched him."

"And the disappointment of losing Nancy," Chris added.

It was fine and quite warm on Saturday for the swimming party. Steve's dad drove them to Paul's house and they planned to walk home.

There was a great deal of noise and splashing going on as they walked round the side of the house and cries of hello as they approached the pool.

The water sparkled in the sunshine and looked inviting. Chris took off a shoe and dabbled her toe in. It felt cold.

"It's fine when you get in," said Paul. "You can go and change in the downstairs cloakroom."

"I've got my trunks on," said Steve, beginning to strip off his jeans and T-shirt.

Why hadn't she thought of that? Chris ran to the house and went in to look for the cloakroom. There was no one about. A big grandfather clock in the hall ticked away slowly but otherwise there was silence. She wondered where Paul's parents were.

Steve was already in the pool when she emerged. Everyone seemed to be absorbed in splashing and diving and took no notice of her so she just sat on the edge and dangled her legs in the water. It was true, after a while it didn't feel cold at all.

She glanced back towards the house again.

"Don't look so worried," said Paul, "Come on in."

Chris looked down at him and now noticed that Sarah Gordon was one of the swimmers. She was standing next to Paul and smiling challengingly up at Chris.

Chris tried to look nonchalant and said, "Your parents not at home, Paul?"

With a sinking feeling she saw him shake his head. "Just gone out to the garden centre. Why? Don't you think we should be left alone? Someone might drown or something?"

Sarah laughed and flung back her head so that her long hair swirled around her.

Chris said nothing. What could she say? That she was not allowed to swim unless there was an adult present? That it was dangerous for her to swim without help at hand? She swung her legs and splashed a little and smiled. How could she get out of this one? What excuse could she give? She should never have come, it would have been easier to make an excuse then than now. Could she pretend to be ill or something?

She was saved making any decision by a sudden tug on her legs, and the next thing she knew was the shock of cold water and the swirl and splash as she sank beneath the surface.

For a moment she was aware of the chlorine stinging her eyes and of the blue tiled walls, and then everything went hazy.

Many hands grabbed at her, pulled her along, heaved her out of the water and she lay on the grass gasping.

"Is she all right?" She recognised Steve's voice and heard the fear in it. "You idiot, Sarah!"

She opened her eyes to see half a dozen worried faces looking down on her.

"I'm OK." She struggled to sit up. "I just have these... I get dizzy sometimes. I'll be all right."

"Shall I phone your parents?" asked Paul.

"No!" she exclaimed. "No thanks, Paul. I'm all right. Really. It was just the shock, the cold water and the surprise and everything."

She remained sitting on the grass as they all got back into the pool. Sarah lingered a little and then, as if with an effort, said quietly, "I'm sorry, Chris."

Chris nodded. "And what about the other thing?" she said.

"What other thing?"

"The cow's eye?"

Sarah looked genuinely puzzled. "The one we dissected in school?"

"No, the one you sent me in the post."

Sarah gasped and knelt down on the grass beside Chris. "I never did that!"

"Someone did."

"It wasn't me, honestly! I would never do a thing like that!"

Chris believed her. No one could pretend that well. "OK. Sorry I suspected you."

Sarah shrugged and got back into the water.

Chris told Steve on the way home.

He nodded. "I said it couldn't be her. She's not that nasty."

"Then I wish I knew who it was and what I've done to them to deserve that."

Steve stopped suddenly and turned to her.

"I know! It must have been Tony Benson! Remember how he pushed you at the ice rink and then threatened you if you didn't mind your own business?"

Chris stared at him silently. But what did Tony mean? Mind her own business. *Was* it the letters? The sooner they were returned to Mr Bingley the better, but how could he know about them? They had been sealed in the wall for years and only she and Steve knew about them.

"Are you sure you never mentioned the letters to anyone?"

Steve looked hurt. "Of course not!"

Chris sighed. Tony Benson *must* be getting her mixed up with someone else and the only way to put and end to this was to confront him at school on Monday.

On Sunday they went to the house again. It had occurred to Chris that if it was the letters Tony meant, then why wasn't he going after Steve as well? He was in it as much as she was.

The baby owls were moving about more on the shelf and

suddenly seemed larger than before, now that they were standing up and spreading their wings, than they did when they were huddled in the nest. Perhaps, after all, they would be able to fly before the demolition started.

Steve had already seated himself on the window ledge as Chris took out the fifth letter. It, too, was different, but where the paper from Nancy's was fine and decorated, this was just scrappy and, in places, grubby and creased.

British Expeditionary Forces

30th December 1914

Dear Ron,
Nancy tells me she's written and told you what she thinks. I warned you, didn't I, and I must say I agree with her. It's hard to call a friend a coward, though, and perhaps I wouldn't go as far as that.

Can't tell you where I am, of course, but must tell you about Christmas Day. By the way, I hope you had a pleasant one!

Well, here it was amazing! On Christmas morning we were in a trench only a few yards from the Germans and there seemed to be a sort of cease fire. One of our officers climbed up and looked out and there were the Germans beckoning to us! Could have been a trick, mind you, but the next thing they were all shouting and waving and we climbed out of the trenches and swapped cigarettes and chocolates with them! They were particularly keen on having some English jam! One of their officers took some photos and then we all linked arms and sang carols, them in German of course! They seemed very friendly. My school German came in handy.

Some of their chaps had been killed during the night so we helped them to bury them and they said: "Thank you, English friends." And so it went on the whole day. What a relief not to hear those guns pounding constantly. Cold day it was, frosty but no snow.

We all recieved a card from the King and cigarettes and

*tobacco in a lovely box from Princess Mary. Wasn't that
thoughtful?*

*Nothing much has happened since then. Perhaps they'll settle
this thing and we can all go home soon.*

*Your friend,
Stanley*

"How sad," said Chris.

"Daft," said Steve. "You're either enemies or you're not.
You can't have a jolly Christmas day with presents and
everything and then start killing each other again."

"Well they did."

"I wonder if it was like that every Christmas."

Chris shrugged. "Don't know."

Steve leaned over to look at the bundle of letters in Chris's
hand. "How many more are there?"

She counted. "Three."

"Read another one then."

She unfolded the next one and began.

British Expeditionary Forces

16th March 1916

Dear Ron,
*Sorry for not writing at all last year but I was wounded at Ypres
and in hospital for six months and unable to write. My right
arm is still not working properly as you can see by this terrible
scrawl, however they consider I'm able to hold a rifle and I'm
being posted next week.*

*Well, Ron, you've got out of it so far but now they've voted
for conscription you'll have to come. Don't be in too much of a
hurry, old chap, but we desperately need more men. The losses
here are appalling. All the pals I joined up with are dead, some
from dysentery and the like, but most in battle.*

There's never been a war like this, Ron. The conditions in the trenches are unbelievable. Standing in freezing mud and water knee-deep so that eventually your feet rot, and the rats…

I'm sorry, Ron, I shouldn't be telling you all this but perhaps it's best you know what you're in for.

To change the subject a little, we heard you've been having bombing raids from Zeppelins over your way and even in London. Hope you're all right.

Nancy and Mother have both been working for the past year, Nancy as a cab driver and Mother in a munitions factory like you. You say they've converted your skating rink?

I'll continue writing to that address in the hope that someone will forward your mail.

Good luck,
Stanley

"Zeppelins," said Chris. "It's a funny name, isn't it?"

"Named after the guy who invented them," said Steve.

"Your dad again?" Chris smiled.

"Yes. You ask one question and you get a lecture."

"Well, no wonder Mr Bingley goes on about Zeppelins if they used to bomb around here. They must have been scary."

"Shall we read another letter?"

"Can't," said Chris, looking at her watch. "It's five o'clock and I've still got some history homework to do."

"Pity it's not First World War."

Chris spun round to him and laughed. "Yes! We'd be top of the class! Goodbye owls!" She threw them a wave as they went through the attic door.

Chapter 4

She sought out Tony Benson during lunch break the next day. Not without her heart thudding and her mouth dry with apprehension. Not without wishing she was anywhere but here. She'd tried to talk herself out of it but, in the end, it was better this way rather than waiting to see what he would do next.

He was with his mates as she'd known he would be. Surrounded by them. They were away over by the gym, kicking a coke can around the grass and talking and laughing in the extra loud voices his sort always have.

Chris took a deep breath and marched up to them.

"Tony!" she called, her voice sounded weak and timid, not at all as she'd intended.

They all spun round and stared at her. Then Tony spoke.

"Yeah?"

"Could I talk to you please?"

Tony grinned. "She wants to talk to me?" he said. His mates all pretended to fall about laughing.

"You are talking to me," he said.

"On your own."

Tony sauntered forward until he was very close. "I got no secrets from me mates. So talk."

"I just want to know what you've got against me," she said. "Why you keep threatening me."

"I?" he mockingly pointed to himself, "Keep threatening

you?" He turned to the others. "Now would I do that?"

The others laughed again. Tony turned back to Chris.

"You know perfectly well what I mean."

"But…" began Chris. "I don't…. about minding my own business…"

"You know what I mean," he repeated, putting his face closer to hers, menacingly. "You say one word and I'll have you."

"What are you to Mr Bingley?" she asked.

He frowned. "Mr Bingley? Who's he? Don't be stupid! Just remember what I said. One word and you'll be sorry."

He slouched back to his friends and left Chris staring after him. So it was nothing to do with the letters, but apart from that she was no wiser.

Disappointed, she walked back to her classroom. She'd gone through all that for nothing.

Sarah seemed nicer to her since the swimming pool incident. Chris asked her again about Bobby.

"Oh, he's fine now," Sarah smiled. "He's a tough little dog."

They both stared out of the classroom window at the dark sky and pouring rain.

"Just as well we went swimming last Saturday," said Sarah. "Looks as though winter's here."

"Just what I was thinking," replied Chris.

"Except that you didn't swim," said Sarah. "Do you often get dizzy like that? You ought to go to the doctor's."

Chris smiled and nodded. "The doctor knows."

"And what is it?"

Chris looked at Sarah's friendly face. Then she

remembered what she had been like earlier. She couldn't be trusted just yet.

"He says I might grow out of it."

Sarah laughed and flicked her hair back.

"They always say that when they can't do anything," she said, packing up her books. "I'll walk home with you."

Chris had expected that she and Steve would go to the house again after school. Now that Sarah was there it made it awkward. Steve was nowhere to be seen, however, so the two of them walked home together.

The next day he explained.

"Sorry! I forgot to tell you I had to stay and audition for a part in the play."

"You! An actor!"

He looked indignant. "Yes, why not?"

"Did you get it?" she asked.

"I don't know yet. Anyway, can we go to the house this afternoon?"

"No, I've got to go with Mum and get a new pair of school shoes and then I'm having a music lesson this evening. Mum's found me a teacher. I used to have lessons before we moved."

"Well, tomorrow, then."

"OK."

But something happened on Wednesday morning. Chris got up and had breakfast as usual, and was about to set off for school when she had the funny feeling again, the warning sign, and worse than before. One minute she was grabbing her school bag and the next thing she knew she woke up lying on the hall floor with her mother bending over her.

41

"You'd better come back to bed, that was a bad one. Have you been taking your tablets regularly?"

Chris nodded, struggling to her feet.

"I'll phone your teacher and say you're sick today. Are you sure you've been all right recently?"

Chris nodded again. It didn't do to tell her mother everything, she fussed too much.

"If it happens again you'll have to see the doctor."

Just as well it hadn't happened at school, thought Chris. That's what she dreaded most.

She was all right for the rest of the week though she hardly saw Steve at all. He'd got the part in the play and they were doing rehearsals, and somehow the week went by without any chance of getting to the house. Chris wondered how the owls were but she'd promised not to go without Steve, at least, she'd promised not to read any more letters without him there. She could always go and see the owls on her own.

In the end she didn't, though. Somehow the house seemed more sinister and she still had a fear that Tony Benson might see her go in and follow.

On Saturday Steve phoned her.

"You haven't been and read any more letters, have you?" he demanded.

"I promised I wouldn't. Where have you been? I haven't seen you for ages. Can you come this afternoon?"

"No, I promised Dad I'd help get things ready for the car boot sale tomorrow."

"The what?"

"You know what car boot sales are. We're going to one tomorrow, selling a lot of old stuff. I've got to sort out some of my old things."

42

"I don't believe you're interested in those letters any more."

"Yes, I am!" he said, crossly. "Look, I wish I could come but I can't."

"What about tomorrow afternoon then?" said Chris. "Car boot sales don't last all day."

"I'll try. I'll give you a ring."

Chris put down the phone crossly. She'd been looking forward to going to the house but Steve seemed to be making every excuse not to go. This whole week he'd been busy doing something else. Well, she'd give him until tomorrow afternoon and then she was going alone.

But the next afternoon she waited and waited for him to call until it was too late to go anywhere. She realised she'd been doing nothing much all weekend and now had all her homework to catch up on.

Strangely enough, the subject of the house came up that evening. It was an eyesore, her mother said. Hadn't been looked after.

"It's going to be demolished soon," said Chris, over-hearing as she came down to get a sandwich.

"Tomorrow," said her father.

Chris stopped, her heart sinking like a heavy weight in her chest.

"T...tomorrow?" she said.

"Chris, are you all right?" asked her mother. "You do look pale."

Chris was staring at her father. "Did you say they were starting tomorrow, Dad?"

Her father peered at her. "What's it to you, Chris?"

"Oh," she shrugged. "Nothing... just interested."

43

"If what I heard is correct, yes, tomorrow."

Chris forgot about her sandwich and wandered back up to her room in a daze, racking her brains as to what she should do. Somehow she had to get there tonight and see if the owls had gone, as well as to rescue the letters. But it was half past eight now. Her parents would never let her go out this late. It would have to be afterwards, later, when they thought she was asleep.

She ran downstairs again, picked up the phone and dialled Steve's number.

"But I can't go out later," Steve said. "Someone would hear me. We could go early tomorrow morning."

"That's no good!" pleaded Chris. "Workmen start early. They might be there at seven or something. It's got to be tonight. You're scared to go at night, aren't you?"

"No! I'm not! It's just that I can't see what you can do if the owls are still there."

Chris wasn't sure either, but she could phone the RSPB.

"How could you live with it on your conscience, not knowing whether the owls got out or were crushed to death in the rubble?" she demanded.

"OK," sighed Steve. "What time?"

"It'll have to be after Mum and Dad go to bed. Let's say midnight?"

"Midnight!"

"I'll see you there." She put the phone down before he could protest further. He wouldn't let her down, she knew.

At ten to twelve Chris crept downstairs, carefully lifted a set of keys off the hook by the front door and let herself out. It was a full moon, or almost, and not at all cold. As she approached the gate of the old house the roar of a car broke the silence. As it sped past something flashed into her mind but immediately went again as she saw Steve waving to her from inside the gate.

"Nearly got caught," he said, excitedly. "Our stairs creak."

Chris saw his eyes glint in the moonlight. Now he was here he was enjoying it.

They opened the attic door and went in. Steve had thought to bring a torch. He shone it over towards the shelf. It was empty.

At first Chris thought perhaps the parent owls were out hunting and that the babies were crouching somewhere out of sight, but when they went closer there was no sign of them.

She sighed. "I'm glad they've gone," she said, "but I never said goodbye." She turned back towards the door.

"Wait!" said Steve. "Don't forget the letters!"

Chris turned back. "I nearly did forget about them!"

"We can take them to Mr Bingley tomorrow."

"There are still two more to read," she said.

"Well, let's read them now."

The beam of his torch swung round towards the wall cupboard.

"What's that?" Chris bent to pick up something off the floor. It was a white feather, but not a long hen's feather like the one in the letter. This was small and soft from the under parts of an owl.

"Another white feather," she said softly, and put it carefully into her pocket.

They perched on the window ledge out of habit and Steve handed Chris his torch.

British Expeditionary Forces

5th July 1917

Dear Ron,

*Why on earth didn't you tell me that you were exempt from
military service? Here we were calling you all sorts of names
and all the time your condition prevented you from serving. I
know you would have if you could. It must be awful having to
put up with all the pressure to join. Why don't you tell people?
It's nothing to be ashamed of, old chap, it's an illness. I must say
we were never aware of you having any seizures. Do let it be
known. Tell people and then they'll know the reason.*

*What was that other thing you talked of? You had to prove
you weren't a coward? I didn't quite understand but anyhow,
you don't have to prove that to anyone. Don't go doing anything
dangerous just to prove a point.*

*Things don't get any better here. I had a bout of dysentery
but got over it all right, thank God. It's a rotten war, Ron, and
it's gone on much longer than anyone imagined, hasn't it? Men
are dying like flies, literally like flies. You can't imagine the
absolute horror of it all.*

*We've been on the march for six weeks! Can you believe it?
Six weeks on the road. In all that time we rarely had the
opportunity to wash and we had one change of clothes. Doesn't
do much good though. Although they fumigate the clothes the
nits survive so, before long, you're alive with the wretched
things again!*

*I hope to get to see you on my next leave – if I get any. In the
meantime, take care and no heroics. Oh, by the way, did you
know that Nancy got married last January? Some officer she met
when he was on leave. He just hailed a cab and it happened to be
hers. Funny how things work out, isn't it? I'm still sorry it
wasn't you and she though.*

Your friend,
Stanley

Chris shuddered and put the letter back in the bundle, then scratched her arm.

"Ugh! Imagine all those lice!"

Steve didn't answer but suddenly put his finger up to his lips. Chris raised her eyebrows questioningly but said nothing. Then she heard it. A creaking on the stairs below.

If she'd been afraid that first day when Steve had followed her, it was nothing compared with now. It was past midnight and dark and they were in an old house some distance from its neighbours. What's more, their parents thought they were asleep in bed.

She clutched Steve's hand.

The creaking stopped and they could feel the presence of someone just outside the door. Their eyes fastened on the handle but it didn't turn. Instead, they heard the sound of the key in the lock. Then someone sniggered and ran back down the stairs. Out in the front garden a figure appeared. It stopped and looked up at them. In the moonlight they could see that he was still laughing and holding up something shiny.

It was Tony Benson and he had the attic key!

Chapter 5

Steve rushed over and tried the door but, of course, it was locked, as they knew very well. Chris couldn't see his face in the darkness but could feel the fear and tension between them in the brief silence.

At last he whispered, "What are we going to do?"

Chris had got over the initial shock.

"Nothing we can do except wait until morning and then shout out of the window. It's no good doing that now, no one would hear us."

He didn't reply but sat down on the floor under the window.

"At least it's not the middle of winter," she said.

"Why did he do that?" mumbled Steve. Then she felt him turn to look at her. "It's your fault! It's you he's after."

"I know, but I've no idea why. I asked him the other day but he still didn't tell me. He just said I knew, and I don't."

"You asked him?"

"Yes. At school on Monday."

She could feel that his mood had changed.

"Sorry I blamed you," he said.

"Let's read the last letter. Then we'll try and get some sleep on this hard floor."

Steve handed her the torch again and she took the final letter out of the bundle.

British Expeditionary Forces

21st March 1918

Dear Ron,
Your letters took ages to reach me and I received them both together.

Are you mad? Ron, you don't have to prove your bravery to anyone. Get rid of it, I beg you! What a thing to do! It could go off at any time! Think of your neighbours. Those things can do a lot of damage to surrounding properties as well as your own. Please Ron, call the police, call someone, but get it out of your house as soon as possible!

There isn't much news from this end. None that I can say, anyway. There aren't words to describe what it's like here. A hell on Earth. It can't go on much longer.

Ron, we'll have some good times once this is over! You'll come up to London and we'll go and see some shows and I'll try to forget this nightmare ever happened – if that's possible.

Take care of yourself – and that means getting rid of that thing you're keeping in your attic.

Fondest regards,
Stanley

Chris jumped up and ran to the broken cupboard, shining the torch inside.

"This must be what he means. This metal thing. Ron never did get rid of it. What is it?"

She heard a sudden gasp behind her and the scrabbling sound of Steve getting to his feet in a hurry and coming over.

"I know what it is." His voice was so soft that she could hardly hear.

"What?" she asked, impatiently.

"It's a bomb!"

Chris jumped back from the cupboard. "A bomb! Don't be

silly. It doesn't look like one. Why should he keep a bomb?"

"Can't you see?" said Steve. "Everyone calling him a coward because he didn't go and fight, Nancy sending him the white feather. Probably she wasn't the only one either. He wanted to prove that he wasn't a coward so he found this unexploded bomb, brought it home and put it in this cupboard."

"You mean he lived with it there all this time?" said Chris, incredulously. "For seventy-five years he lived in a house with a bomb in it?"

"Yes."

"Do you think it could go off at any time?" She shivered.

"I suppose so. I expect they get more unstable the older they are."

"Thanks," she said, "You're very cheerful."

"It's unlikely to go off tonight just because we're here." He grabbed her arm suddenly. "But what about when they demolish the house!"

"That's what I was thinking."

"What was wrong with old Ron Bingley, then? I can't remember the word that Stanley used."

"Seizures."

"Yeah, that's it."

"He was epileptic," she said.

"You mean he had fits?"

"That's what seizures are. We... seizures means fits."

"I remember there was a kid at school used to have fits." said Steve. "Everyone used to take the mickey. He never had many friends. I think people thought they might catch it or something."

"Now you know why Mr Bingley was thought weird or even mad. Things get exaggerated."

"Yeah. Poor old guy."

"Steve."

"Yes?"

Chris took a deep breath. "I'm epileptic."

"You are?" She could feel his eyes on her.

"You know I was off school this week? It's because I had a bad seizure."

She could tell that Steve couldn't think what to say.

"How do you stop them?" he managed at last.

"I take tablets." As soon as she said it a horrible thought hit her. Had she taken her bedtime tablets? She didn't remember doing so in all the worry over the owls. She'd taken them upstairs with a glass of water but couldn't remember actually swallowing them.

She voiced her thoughts. "I can't remember whether I took my night-time tablets. You'd better know what to do in case I have a seizure."

Steve said nothing.

"Don't worry," she said, "It looks worse than it is. And you don't have to do anything really, just make sure I'm lying down and put your jacket or something under my head. When I stop moving, roll me on to my side and then I'll just sleep for a while."

"I hope you don't have one," said Steve, anxiously.

"I probably won't, but now I've told you so you won't panic. Anyway, that's a more serious one. Sometimes I just sort of go blank for a few seconds – like at the swimming pool, only that happened when I was under water."

Steve grunted, as if understanding better.

"You should tell everyone about it. It's worse if you have a seizure and they don't know what it is."

She nodded. "I suppose so."

"You're like Ron. Afraid to tell anyone, and it didn't do him much good."

"They still don't understand. I've been through it all before at my other school. Calling me awful names and afraid to come near me."

"What causes it, anyhow?"

"It's something to do with messages in the brain going the wrong way."

They didn't speak about it any more but settled down to try and get comfortable and wait for dawn. Neither slept much. They had too much on their minds. The bomb in the cupboard just a few metres away, the possibility of Chris having a seizure, and the workmen arriving early and starting up their demolition machinery.

When it began to get light they sat on the window sill, watching for any passers-by they could shout to. But it was early still, and no one was about.

"We have to get out before the workmen arrive," said Steve, "otherwise no one will hear us shouting then."

Several cars passed but that was useless. The attic was bare, so they didn't even have anything to wave with or throw out of the window.

"We could throw out the letters," suggested Steve, "someone might see them fluttering down."

"No!" said Chris, adamantly. She grabbed the bundle of letters and stuffed them into her pocket. "I'm going out on to the roof."

"You're what?"

"Look!" she pointed. "There's a little ledge outside this window and it leads to a flat area of roof. If we could get to that we'd be seen more easily."

"You're mad!" said Steve. "Anyway, you might have a seizure."

"I'll just have to hope I don't."

"Now you're doing the same as Ron. Trying to prove your bravery!"

"I am not!" said Chris. "I just want us to get out of here!"

"I'll go," said Steve, quietly.

Chris looked at him and saw that it wasn't just bravado. He meant it. They opened the window and he climbed up on to the ledge and then carefully stepped through.

His knuckles were white as he gripped the window frame and carefully put one foot out on to the narrow ledge. The other foot followed and he edged his way along towards the flat square of roof just a few metres away. Then he stopped.

"What's the matter?" asked Chris.

"There's nothing to hold on to just here," Steve said, his voice shaking. "I can't quite reach."

Chris looked. A few centimetres beyond Steve's outstretched arm was a ridge of tiling which, if he could reach it, would help him on to the roof.

"I'm coming," said Chris. "If I hold the edge of the window with one hand and your hand with the other, you should be able to reach."

He didn't protest this time. He could see it was the only way. Chris climbed out and slowly stepped along the ledge. Steve took her other hand and moved further, reached out, and grabbed the ridge of tiles. Then, in no time, he was on

the flat roof, helping her to come after him.

"We made it!" They both laughed with relief.

"There's still nobody around. He looked at his watch. "It's a quarter to eight. My mum'll be in a panic wondering where I am."

"So will mine!"

"There's someone!" Steve suddenly shouted. "Look!" He pointed over the side of the house. "It's a man walking along that side road."

They both started shouting and waving madly. For some time the man seemed not to hear. Then, all at once, he looked up and stopped. He shaded his eyes with his hand and continued to stare.

"Help us!" they shouted. "We're trapped up here!"

The man turned around and began to walk away again.

"He's not in any hurry," said Chris. "He's walking as if we've got all day."

The traffic along the road in front was getting quite heavy now but no one saw the two of them, up on the roof. Then there was the man again, and someone else with him. They both waved and shouted something indistinguishable, and then the second person hurried away again leaving the man standing there, just staring up at them.

Within ten minutes it was all happening. First a police car arrived, then a fire engine, followed by the demolition workmen in their heavy machinery. Soon a long ladder was extending up towards them.

"I'm not going down on that!" said Chris firmly.

"It's the quickest way," said Steve. "They'll never break down that thick attic door."

Quite a crowd had gathered below, all faces staring

upward. Chris wondered if either of their parents were among them. It was strange being the centre of attention. She wondered if she'd be in awful trouble when she got home.

"Do you feel all right?" asked Steve, looking worried.

Chris sighed. "You're as bad as my mum. Don't you start fussing."

He said nothing but looked at the long ladder coming up towards them and she knew what he was thinking. If she had a seizure while going down the ladder…

A fireman climbed over the edge of the roof.

"You kids all right? How'd you get trapped up here?"

"Someone locked us in."

"What were you doing up here, anyway?"

"It's a long story," said Steve.

The fireman looked at him. "Well, you'd best tell it to the police when you get down. Some old boy down there says there's a bomb in the building."

"There is."

"Right then," said the fireman, calmly. "Now, I'll start down first and you two come after me. Don't look down. Not afraid of heights, are you?"

"No!" they both said, hearts thudding, and began the slow descent of the ladder.

It wasn't really so high, thought Chris, half way down now. She was beginning to enjoy it a little and was very aware of the sea of faces watching their progress.

They reached the ground and Chris thanked the fireman. Two police officers were waiting to talk to them.

"What were you two doing up in that building? Didn't you know it was going to be demolished today?"

Chris nodded. "We went to see if the owls had gone." She explained about the owls and then about being locked in.

"Any idea who locked you in?" The policeman sounded slightly disbelieving.

"Yes," said Steve. "It was Tony Benson. We saw him as he left."

"In the dark?"

"It was moonlight," said Chris.

"Now why should this Tony Benson want to lock you in?" asked the policeman, still looking sceptical.

"We don't know," said Steve, "but he keeps threatening Chris."

The policeman shook his head. "Well someone locked you in, that's certain. The door's locked and the key's gone."

"It was Tony Benson," insisted Steve. "We heard the key turn in the lock and the back door close. Then he looked up and we could see him in the moonlight, holding up the key. It was Tony Benson."

"He's right," said someone behind them and they turned to see Mr Gordon pushing through the small crowd.

"Did you see him then, Sir?" asked the policeman.

"No, but I know why he was threatening Chris, here. She was a witness to a crime he had committed."

"Was I?" asked Chris, surprised.

Mr Gordon smiled at her. "You remember when you rescued our Bobby after he'd been hit by a car?"

She nodded.

"That was young Tony Benson. I've seen him since. Evidently 'borrows' his mum's car."

Mr Gordon faced the policeman again. "Aged fifteen," he

said. "No licence, no insurance, and he hit a dog and no doubt didn't report it. Chris here saw him but didn't recognise him – she's new to the area. But Tony recognised her and thought she would give him away. That would explain the threats to keep her quiet."

The policeman nodded. "I see," he said. "Right, Sir. Thank you. We'll go and have a talk with the lad. Now, apart from that, what's this about a bomb?"

"There is a bomb in a cupboard," said Steve, excitedly. "A First World War bomb."

"And how do you know that?"

Steve looked at Chris. "Er, well… it looks old…" he said, lamely.

"We'll go and have a look," said the policeman. "Now there's no need for you all to hang about!" he addressed the crowd. "You can all go!" He strode off around the back of the house with his partner. No one else moved.

"There's Mr Bingley!" whispered Steve, nudging Chris. She looked across to see an elderly man staring up at the house.

"That's the man who went for help when we shouted," she said.

"Are you sure?"

"Yes, I remember the cap. Let's go and talk to him."

Steve hung back a little.

"Come on!" urged Chris.

As they approached the old man they could hear him muttering.

"Mr Bingley?" said Chris. He didn't appear to hear her but continued gazing up towards the top of the house. Chris put her hand on his arm.

"Mr Bingley?"

This time he jumped slightly and turned to peer at her.

"Thank you for going to get help," she said.

He smiled and nodded, then resumed his upward gaze, frowning. "The bomb," he said.

"Don't worry," said Chris, "the police will take it away, but I have your letters here safe."

He looked back at her. Chris pulled the bundle out of her pocket and held them out to him.

He took them slowly, turning them over in his hands and holding them closer to his face.

"My letters from Stanley," he said, quietly.

Chris nodded.

"Did you read them?" he asked. There was life in his eyes now, a sort of excitement, not accusing, but eager. Chris, nevertheless, still felt ashamed.

"Yes," she said. "I didn't know they were yours at first."

He nodded but said nothing. There was silence between them for a while and they stared back at the house again.

"I'm epileptic too," she said at last.

The old man looked at her again. "You understand then," he said.

"Yes."

Steve had said nothing all this time but he now spoke.

"What happened to Stanley?" he asked.

Mr Bingley's old eyes drooped a little. "Killed at the Somme," he said, "just after that last letter. Twenty-one he was, just twenty-one."

"Poor Stanley," said Chris, not knowing what else to say.

It was all a long time ago but she could see that the old man was still sad about it. He held up the bundle of letters.

"Would you come to the home sometime and read these to me?" he asked. "My eyes aren't so good nowadays."

"Of course!" said Chris.

Mr Bingley nodded. "Well, I'm off before they start asking me about the bomb," he said. "Everyone already thinks I'm crackers." With a toothless grin he shuffled away.

Steve looked at Chris. "The police know it was him. Everyone knows it was his house and bombs don't drop into cupboards."

"I know," said Chris, "but I don't expect they'll do anything. He's an old man."

The two policemen emerged from the house just then and one of them went straight to the patrol car. The other came up to Chris and Steve.

"I don't know how you kids knew that was a bomb," he said. "It doesn't look like you expect a bomb to look."

They said nothing.

"However," he continued, "that daft old Mr Bingley has been going on about bombs for years, apparently. Must have hoarded it there himself." He shook his head in disbelief. "Now why should anyone do that?" He looked at the two who stared back at him innocently.

"I expect he had a good reason," said Chris.

"Good reason? You tell me one good reason for keeping a bomb in the attic of your house for eighty years."

Steve shrugged.

"Putting the whole neighbourhood in danger too," went on the policeman, shaking his head. "There's some funny people about."

His colleague approached. "I've been on to bomb disposal," he said, "They say it sounds like a World War One fifty kilogram Carbonit bomb dropped by Zeppelins. They want the whole area evacuated."

Within half an hour the police had been round the nearby streets in a car with a loud hailer and moved everyone out of their houses to beyond a cordoned-off area.

Steve's house was one of those within the danger area. His dad had already gone to work, but as his mum and younger brother came out of the front door he ran up to them.

"Steve! I was worried to death about you!" cried his mum.

"I'll explain it all later," he said.

"You'll be late for school!"

Steve looked horrified. "Go to school and miss this?"

"I'd better go and tell my parents," said Chris, and sped off.

They were both in the kitchen when she arrived and breathlessly burst in through the back door.

"Chris!" Her mum looked pale and worried. "Where have you been this early?

"It's the old house!" panted Chris, excitedly.

"You keep away," growled her dad, "it's dangerous hanging round demolition sites."

"There's a bomb in it! The bomb disposal people are coming. They've cleared the streets. I'll be back soon."

She turned and fled back out of the door before they could say anything more. She wasn't going to miss this for anything. There might be trouble later but at least they thought she'd just gone out early and didn't realise she'd been out all night!

Chris and Steve watched excitedly from as close as they

could. They were out of sight of the house but, somehow, news of what was going on seemed to filter through.

The bomb disposal unit had arrived and gone into the house. There was speculation as to whether they would defuse it where it was, detonate it, or take it away for detonation. It was soon evident that they must be defusing it.

"What a job," someone said. "It could go off at any moment."

Chris tried to visualise what was going on. She'd seen a film not long ago where a bomb had to be defused. She remembered the care with which the man had slowly unscrewed the casing. Then he had lifted it off and been faced with lots of wiring which he had to carefully cut. But would this bomb be like that? She didn't know, only that it was very old and rusty, unlike the one in the film.

No one spoke much. The courage and skill of one man was being tested at this moment and his life depended on it. Everyone was thankful they weren't in his shoes.

At last a sigh of relief swept through the onlookers as word got through that it was done. The bomb was safe. As the two men from the Royal Engineers bomb disposal unit drove away, applause broke out in the crowd.

Chris looked at Steve. "Well, that's the end of that."

He nodded. "It was a good secret, wasn't it? Are you really going to go and read those letters to Mr Bingley?"

"Yes. I'll go this afternoon after school."

"School!" said Steve. "I suppose we'd better go now."

"Not until I've had some breakfast!"

Chris had come to a decision earlier and she acted upon it that lunchtime by going to see the Head. In the afternoon a special assembly was called and the whole school heard about Chris's epilepsy and what they could do to help if she had a seizure. Everyone seemed interested and helpful, but much more intrigued by the episode of the bomb, and Chris and Steve enjoyed relating the story for the rest of the afternoon, carefully omitting any mention of the letters.

Chris smiled happily to herself as she walked towards the old people's home that afternoon. She felt as if she were walking on air, as if a weight had been lifted from her shoulders. The fact of her epilepsy was out in the open at last. There would still be times when people would taunt her, she knew, or be afraid if she had a seizure, but at least now they would be aware of what was happening. For the first time she did not feel afraid of others' reactions to her epilepsy: she felt accepted.

Mr Bingley sat in an armchair in a corner of the sitting room with Chris beside him.

"Dear Ron," she began…